Photographic guide book of

minorca

Photography • **Marc Pons**

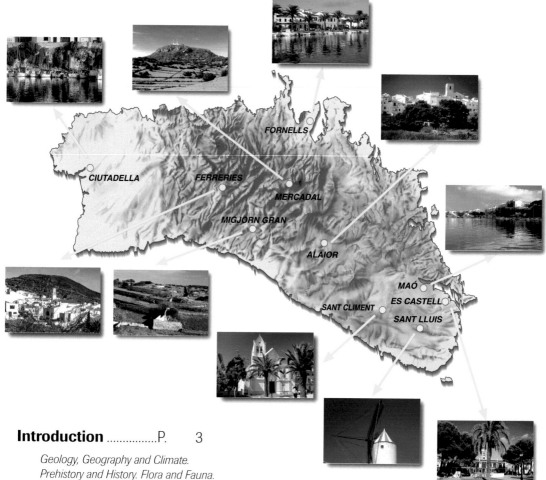

FORNELLS

CIUTADELLA

FERRERIES

MERCADAL

MIGJORN GRAN

ALAIOR

MAÓ

ES CASTELL

SANT CLIMENT

SANT LLUIS

3rd UPDATED EDITION

Published by: Llum del Mediterrani Postals
Photography: Marc Pons
    Photo pág. 8 with kind permission of GOB Menorca
    Photo pág. 8 with kind permission of José Almagro
    Photos págs. 42 & 69 with kind permission of Pedro Florit
Translated by: Nicholas Nabokov
Design: Trivium Serveis Publicitaris, S.L.
Printed by: Sanvergràfic. S.L.
D. Legal: B.27.576-2006
ISBN: 84-607-2350-x

First of all, welcome to our beautiful island. It is hoped that you will take full advantage of your holiday and have a relaxing time.

This guide-book, published after more than a year of compiling and selecting the best photos, aims to give you information on the most beautiful places to visit during your stay in Minorca.

Each photo has a description that will be very useful, with interesting information on locations selected, access and characteristics.

Each chapter of this guide-book is dedicated to a town and points out its most interesting aspects. At the start of each chapter, you will find a map which indicates access routes and points of interest.

At the bottom of each photo you will find a number that precisely indicates the location on the map and on the street map that appears at the end of each chapter.

The beginning of the guide-book is made up of a brief introduction that informs the reader on interesting aspects of the island, such as geology, geography, climate, its economy and gastronomy and its rich flora and fauna. There is also a short summary on its history.

Words written in **bold** are typical Minorcan words, written in the island's own dialect. Lastly, we hope you enjoy this photographic guide-book as much as we did in compiling it.

Presentation

Minorca, the most easterly and northerly of the Balearic Islands, offers its visitors a variety of landscapes and prehistoric monuments, something difficult to find in such concentration anywhere else in the world. This island of some 48 km. long by 18 km. wide and located in the heart of the western Mediterranean will not fail to surprise those who seek more than just sun and sand for their holidays.

Minorca is the second largest island of the Balearic Archipelago with 702 sq. mts. The first impression is that it seems flat and its only notable high areas are **Santa Águeda** (264 m.), **s'Enclusa**, (274 m.) with the remains of an American military base at the top and **Monte Toro** (358 m.), none of which can be described as very high. This first impression can only change when an outsider carefully travels around the island and is amazed at the proud cliffs of the north and delights in the natural gullies of the south.

The island offers its 290 km. coastal perimeter to anyone who has the time and desire to travel around it. This could be on foot, using the **Camí de Cavalls**, a centuries old path that goes around the island or by boat, which allows you to visit the most isolated places around its coast. Without a doubt, you will not be disappointed at the beauty you come across.

In geological terms, it is necessary to differentiate between the northern part of the island, with its ancient ground that belongs to the Palaeozoic era (the most ancient area of the Balearics) and the southern part, formed in the Miocene period and whose main material is made up of soft calcareous rock. In this southern part, or **Migjorn**, the action of thousands of years of erosion has resulted in fertile gullies and beaches of fine white sand. On the contrary , the northern part has beaches of reddish sand that contains siliceous material. Also you will find slate and clay that have a colour sequence that goes from reddish earth to grey rocks. The natural boundary between these two zones is the road that links Maó to Ciutadella except for the last stage in which this boundary deviates up to the **Algaiarens** beaches.

The climate is typically Mediterranean, with two dry seasons, summer and winter, and two wet seasons, autumn and spring, with torrential rain. This is why the possibility of having a continuous flow of water is practically zero.

Average temperatures vary from 25º C in summer to 12ºC in winter. The average winter temperature can be considered mild and only the older residents of the island can remember more than one snowfall.

The average rainfall in Minorca is the highest of the Balearic Islands and humidity therefore is very high. This causes the appearance of dew or **banyadura**. The winds that blow and sometimes batter the island are as varied as their provenance. They range from the warm **Migjorn** to the humid **Xaloc** and **Llebeig**, to the strong **Gregal** and **Mestral** and above all the **Tramuntana**, all of which are key elements in popular sayings. La **Tramuntana** is a cold and dry wind that comes from Russia . It reaches the Alps and deviates from there to Minorca, reaching speeds of up to 100 k.p.h.. This sudden wind has caused numerous shipwrecks on the north coast that was christened by the French "The coast of death". The influence of this wind can be seen by looking at the island's trees, most of which lean south.

Prehistoric architecture, present all over the island, is very important both in terms of quantity and excellent state of conservation. Settlements, burial sites, caves, **taules** and **talaiots** can be visited by archaeology lovers.

It is believed that the first inhabitants arrived in Minorca around the year 2000 B. C. from southern France in rafts pushed by the **Tramuntana**. These groups lived in natural caves, that sometimes they enlarged according to their needs, and were usually located in the gullies for protection. The most important groups were those of **Cala Morell**, **Cales Coves**, **Torreta Saura** and **Macarella**. This was the pre-Talayotic era.

From 1400 B. C. we enter the **Talayotic** era, when wooden houses were built and men dedicated themselves to harvesting and pasture. The defensive walls surrounding some settlements date from this period. The word "**talayotic**" comes from **talaiots** that were watch-towers. There are more than 300 of these scattered around the island. Their base can be square, oval or cross-shaped with a height ranging from 4 to 14 metres and either hollow or solid. The **taules** also belong to this period. They are made up of two megalithic "T"-shaped blocks. The most famous are **Trepucó**, **Torralba**, **Torretrencada** and **Talatí**. The number of these monuments amount to roughly thirty. It is not known for sure for what reason they were built, however, it is thought that they have a religious character. Other monuments of this period are the **navetes**, burial sites, like the well known **Naveta de Es Tudons**, located about 3 km. from Ciutadella and visible from the main road. A more detailed description can be found in the chapters dedicated to the municipalities.

Throughout the centuries, Minorca has been occupied by countless outsiders, both peacefully and militarily. The majority of these invaders left their mark on both the landscape of the island and its customs. The island's strategic importance (the port of Maó is one of the biggest natural harbours in the world) and the ease of defending it once conquered

made Minorca an attractive place for invaders throughout the ages. It is believed that the Phoenicians, keen traders from Tyre and Sidon, were the first people to establish contact with the Minorcans. In reality their objectives were the mines of Tarsis in southern Spain and the island was used as a staging post during their journeys. Minorca was called Nura, which meant fire. This was because of the many bonfires on top of the **talaiots** that were visible from the coast. Later the island was visited by the Greeks who left behind remains such as urns and statuettes.

The first military occupation of the island was carried out by the Carthaginians who gave the name of "Magha" to Maó in honour of Hannibal Barca's brother. Minorcan sling-shooters in this period already enjoyed a well deserved fame and for this they were recruited by the army in its conflicts against Rome. This ability with the sling was developed from childhood. Children's food was placed on tree branches and if the food was not knocked down by sling, they did not eat! In 252 B. C. a rebellion against the occupiers took place but this was put down and the rebels received punishments which included crucifixion.

From 123 B. C. the island, like the rest of the Balearics, passed over to Roman domination after an expedition by Quinto Cecilio. Three cities existed then: Magona (Maó), Iammona (Ciutadella) and Sanisera (near Fornells). These three were joined by a Roman road. Remains include engravings, ceramics, coins, and gold and silver articles. From this period until the Muslim domination there was a dark period in which Christianity reached the island and early Christian basílicas were built whose remains can be seen in **Son Bou**, **Fornás de Torrelló** and **Fornells**. Later, Minorca was dominated by Vandals of the Aryan religion, who proved to be very cruel towards Christians. They even assassinated the bishop of Ciutadella, Macario. Around 530 A. D. the island passed over to the Byzantine domination.

The spread of Islam from North Africa arrived

Prehistory – History

in Minorca around the 10th century. The Muslims were tolerant towards the islanders and they allowed them to follow their faith. Ciutadella was named Medina-Minurka and was walled, although the main military enclave was the **Sta. Águeda** fort (Ferreries). Islamic culture had a great influence on the islanders: their love of horses, legends (**Cova de en Xoroi**), and many place-names still in use today.

Let us move on to the year 1232, when the kingdom of Aragón decided to annexe the Balearic Islands. Majorca was conquered and the Moors in Minorca became vassals of James II. Peaceful coexistence continued without problems until there was an attempt at treachery by the Muslims. As a response, in January 1287, troops from Aragón started to land at the harbour of Maó and reached Ciutadella and then the castle of **Santa Águeda** where the Moors capitulated, leaving Minorca under the domination of Aragón and Catalonia. In 1427, Alfonso V resettled prisoners from Catalan jails onto the island. These prisoners received their liberty as settlers and ironically were called "good people from Catalonia". The remains of this period are the **San Roque** gate in Maó, some coastal ramparts and the Ciutadella cathedral.

We now come to 1500 and the island becomes less interesting to the kings of the peninsula, who are more concentrated on discovering the New World . As a result, Minorca became exposed to raids by Turkish pirates of the period. Thus, in 1535, the famous pirate "Barbarossa" brought blood and fire to Maó, taking 600 slaves. The fortunes of its neighbour, Ciutadella, were not much better. In 1558 it suffered a devastating attack by 140 Turkish ships. A large part of the city was destroyed and though the exact number of slaves taken is

unknown, it is thought to be very high. The obelisk in the "Plaza del Borne" was erected in memory of those brave people who were killed or enslaved by the Ottomans. During the 18th century the island once again began to interest the great powers of the period and so, in 1713 as a result of the Utrecht treaty, Minorca passed into British hands. From this period the works of the governor, Richard Kane, stand out. He transferred the capital to Maó and carried out many improvements to the infrastructure such as the **Camí de en Kane** that linked Maó and Ciutadella. A part of this road still exists today. Also outstanding is his reclamation of the marshes in the **Es Pla Verd** area, that became farmland. He lived in the **San Felip** castle and was the only governor to gain respect from the Minorcans. His successors proved to be despotic and cruel and did not contribute in any way to improvements on the island. From 1756 to 1763 the French flag flew over Minorca. A landing of 12,000 soldiers, under the command of the Duke de Richelieu, conquered the island from Ciutadella to the **San Felipe** Castle. The only advantage of the conquest for the Minorcans was easy access to French universities and the only thing the French took away with them was the recipe for mayonnaise!

The second British domination started in 1763 with James Johnston as governor and ended in 1782 when Minorca passed into Spanish hands with the Duke of Crillón as governor. From 1798, the third and last British domination started. During this period the famous admiral Nelson resided in Maó at "Golden Farm", a house situated on the northern part of Maó harbour.

The 1802 peace treaty of Amiens returned the island to Spain who has retained sovereignty to the present day.

Prehistory - History

Minorca was awarded the title of Biosphere Reserve by U.N.E.S.C.O. in 1993. This was due to its unique characteristics and its high level of environmental conservation. In the past few years of increased tourism, the natural wealth of the island has decreased somewhat. However, it is still possible to find areas of great natural value such as virgin beaches and areas designated as A.N.E.I. (Natural Areas of Special Interest) that are protected by law.

The majority of trees here are evergreen. The predominant species is the Mediterranean pine that, as a result of its ease of reproduction and adaptability, has overtaken indigenous species such as oak, olive trees, wild olive trees, carob trees, fig trees etc. The prickly pear tree is known as **figues de moro**. Thickets that intermingle with woods are varied. The most abundant are: lentisks, tree strawberries, brooms and various types of bramble.

As far as flowers are concerned, the intense red of poppies stands out. Also, the Minorcan orchid called **mosca** and the **fel i vinagre** that covers many fields in yellow in Spring. The beaches and the dune areas have their own characteristic flora, made up of brambles, that help in the settlement of the sands, and small trees like savins. Passing on to the animal kingdom, what stands out is the variety of small mammals such as martens, ferrets, weasels, rabbits, bats, mice and the sleepy hedgehogs that we must be careful not to run over as they tend to cross roads or simply sit on roads for the warmth of the tarmac!

There are more Mediterranean tortoises in Minorca than in the neighbouring islands, although the population has been decreasing in recent years as a result of the tortoises' popularity as a pet, which today is prohibited by the conservation laws. There are also reptiles like snakes (non-venomous) and **sargantanes** which are endemic lizards that inhabit the islets that surround the island.

The greatest natural wealth of the island is to be found in the sky. There are royal kites and fish eagles, both extinct in many areas. Here in Minorca they find a safe haven for their survival. Smaller birds of prey like falcons, kestrels and sparrowhawks are easily sighted in all areas. We can also observe the **miloca**, a carrion of which few specimens remain. At nightfall and with a little luck, we can observe the silent flight of the **òliva**, a large owl with a very white plumage.

Close to the cliffs it is easy to observe the common seagull that nests in great numbers like cormorants, "paiños" and pewit gulls. Small birds are also present in large numbers and varieties. Crows, partridges, quails, pigeons, wild pigeons, hoopoes, nighthawks and others all brighten up our views of the Minorcan countryside. Some migratory birds like starlings cross the island each winter and provide a wonderful spectacle in the sky.

Flora and Fauna

The greatest ornithological wealth, however, can be seen in the **de es Grau** lagoon, the first and only nature reserve on the island. Located near Maó, this unique area allows one the possibility of observing a large number of birds such as mallards, coots, water-hens, storks, egrets etc. It is a breeding ground for many migratory birds.

In the fields or **tanques** one can find a large number of cows (some 23,000 on all the island). The majority of these are Friesian cows with their characteristic black and white colouring, although the indigenous cows are a reddish colour. Horses, essential in local fiestas, are jet black and are a breed apart. They are highly prized by horse lovers. Sheep and goats complete the island's livestock.

In the sea and close to the coast, the carpet of Neptune grass houses and sustains a large quantity of small fish known as **peix roquer** that are very tasty. In slightly deeper waters one finds the grouper fish, which is very sought after for its flesh quality, the **escorpra** or scorpion fish, white bream, barracudas, **pagres** etc., that are fished using nets or paternoster lines. Squid and "serrano" (fish similar to grouper) fishing is a tradition among the locals as these two species are found in abundance. Less lucky has been the monk seal or **vell marí** already extinct, or the marine turtle whose survival is evident only when they are sometimes caught in a fisherman's nets.

The sea-floor is mainly rocky and very beautiful, proof of which is that the World Undersea Photographic Competition was held in Ciutadella a few years ago.

Trawlers fill the markets with their products, mainly prawns, crayfish and monkfish. Lobster fishing is also very important and provides work to many fishermen between March and August. Lobster fishing is carried out by means of the old method of **nanses**, which is very selective or with special nets just for this purpose.

Flora and Fauna

Tourism, which came late to the island, has become the main source of income for Minorcans, replacing historical industries such as footwear, leather and fashion jewellery. The great demand for workers in the tourist industry every year provokes an influx of workers that increases the floating population by several thousand people.

"El Caserío" whose factory is located in Maó and is currently owned by a multinational. The remainder of the milk is used mainly for the production of the famous cheese with the denomination of origin of Maó, **queso de Mahón Menorca**, that is always more highly valued.

Agrotourism, which has become fashionable recently, is another source of income for the countryside and it may be a way of rehabilitating the large number of **llocs** (farmhouses) that are in a poor state of repair or abandoned. This may be a way of conserving part of rural Minorcan architecture.

We also find more traditional ways of earning a living. Fishing, centred around trawlers and lobster fishing, rewards us with very beautiful images such as old fishermen repairing their nets and smoking their pipes on the shore of the harbours.

In the harbours of Ciutadella, Maó and Fornells we can see the fishermen setting off at dawn to fish for the fruits of the Mediterranean, that unfortunately are always scarcer, and then sold to local restaurants. The restaurants of Fornells are especially well known for their preparation of the famous "**caldereta de llagosta**" (lobster stew). This dish can also be found in many other restaurants at more affordable prices.

Another typical Minorcan product is **gin** that is distilled in the Gin Xoriguer distillery in the port of Maó. This drink is essential in local Minorcan fiestas.

The shoe industry has gone from a large number of small firms to a small number of larger firms located in the Ciutadella and Ferreries areas. Tourists can visit these firms and buy directly from the factory. The fashion jewellery industry has followed the same route, though its decline has perhaps been greater owing to insular costs and, in the past few decades, increased competition from Asian countries.

Farming is another sector that is still active, mainly for milk-production that is the raw material for cheese portions produced by

Economy and Gastronomy

Ciutadella

PUNTA NATI

Cala Es Pous
Cala Es Morts
Punta Jonc

Ses Capelles
Punta Na Porradell
Cala Be
Punta Espardina
Punta Perpinyà de Fora
Punta Perpinyà de Dins
S'Amarador
Sa Falconera
Ses Busquets
Cap de Bajolí
Es Pont d'En Gil
Els Llebetxats
Cale es
Cap de Banyos

Sa Marina de son Escudero
Son Escudero
Son Bernadí
Son Mascaró
Torre Vella
Son Triai
Son Fe
Son Salomó
St Ignasi
S'Hort d'en Vigo
Rafal d'Es Capità
So n'Anglado
Son Font
Sta Leonor
Son Salvador
Ses Troqueries
St Sebastià
St Nicolau
Son Fedelic
Torre del Ram
Hipòdrom
CALA'N BLANES
Rafal des Con
CIUTADELLA
Polígon Industrial
RONDA NORD
Son Juaneda
Es Caragol
Vila Pons
Hostals
Son Roso
Sa Vinya Gran
Ses Angoixes

Sa Marina de Son Morell
Cala Morell
CALA MORELL
Curniola
Curniola
La Vall
Algairens
Son Morell Nou
Clariana
Biniatram
Son Seu
Son Morell
Torre d'En Quart
Son Pomar
Binigafull
So n'Angel
Ses Arenes de Baix
Es Caragolí
Ses Arenetes
Son Quart
Canal de l'Infern
Son Pebre
Sta Victòria

Muntanya Mala
Falconera, 205 m.
Es Pla de sa Font
S'Hort de la Font Santa
S'Almudaina
Es Pla d'es Camí
Binicanó
S'Almudaina
CASTILLO MENORCA
Alputz
Ses Garrigu
Coll Roig
Ses Tavernes
Son Toni Martí
Sta Margarida
Sa Muntaneta
Santa Magdalena

NAVETA DES TUDONS
Naveta des Tudons
Es Tudons
Sa Vinyeta
Son Sintes
Torre Llafuda
Torre Trencada
Tot Lluch
Torrepetxina
Torre Saura
Son Guillem
Torretó
Son Febrer
Torrepetxina
Son Sarparets
Sobrevе
Es Cana

Sa Coma
St Damianot
Son Quim
son Jordi
Sa Llegítima
Rafal d'es Mores
Son Roseta
Rafal Vell
Binipati Nou
Binigarba
Cavalleria Nova
Torre Llafuda
Cavallerieta
Canavallons
Morvedre Vell
Bellaventura
Tot Lluquet

Cala En Forcat
Cala En Brut
En Blanes
PORT DE CIUTADELLA
SANTANDRIA
Sa Caleta
Cala Santandria
Punta Rafalera
Punta Quintana
Cala Blanca
Punta de S'Aigua Dolça
S'Aigua Dolça
Cala En Bastó
Cap Negre
Sa Bolda de N'Aleix
Cala Xada
Punta des Sac des Blat
Sac des Blat
Barraca de L'Homo
Na Guinavet
Es Secanys
Cap de Mal Passar
S'Extremaunció

SON CARRIÓ
Rafal Amagat
St Antoni
Son Pons
Son Jover
Son Morro
So Na Marineta
So n'Olivaret
So n'Olivar Vell
Sto Domingo
S'Alquerieta Vella
S'Alquerieta Nova
Binibó
Son Catlar
Son Bou Vell
Son Bou Nou
Son Marc
Son Xoriguer Vell
So n'Olivar Nou
St Vicent
St Pere
Son Marquet
Torre Saura Vell
Son Vell
So Na Parets
Son Xoriguer
Son Saura
Es Banyuls

SAN JOAN DE MISSA
St Rosa
Egipte
St Joaner
St Joanet
Llocd'es Pou
Son Foc
Son Tica
Lloc Nou
Morvedre Nou
St Joan Gran
Morvedre
Son Piris
Alpara
Pavordia Nova
Pavordia Vella
Torralbet
Son Mestres Nou
Torralba
Sta Galdana
Sta Maria
Son Mestres de Dalt
Horts de Binissaid
STA GALDANA

SON CATLAR
Son Camaró
So n'Alzina
Sa Marjaleta
Sa Marjal Vella
Sa Marjal Nova
St Francesc
Macarella
Sa Cova
Son Vecete
Son Tarí Nou
Bellavista
Mallauí
Milocar de Santa Anna
Sta Anna
Barranch
Son Tari Vell

CALA EN BOSC
SON XORIGUER
Cala en Bosc
Platjals de So Na Parets
Platjals de Son Xoriguer
S'Anell de Ferro
Es Bol de ses Cirvies
Cala Parejals
Racoada de Son Vell
Cala de Son Vell
Es Melaos
Es Bol de Son Vell
Arenal de Son Saura
En Escalons
Cala des Talaier
Cala En Turqueta
Cala Macarella
Macarelleta
Racó des Mart
Cala Santa Galdana
Cala Miljana
Cala Mitjaneta
Cala en Rafal

CAP D'ARTRUTX
Racó des Bregarol

A *Ciutadella*

TOWN CENTRE

NORTHERN AREA

WESTERN AREA

SOUTHERN AREA

LITHICA - QUARRIES

ARCHAEOLOGICAL AREA

FIESTAS OF SANT JOAN

CIUTADELLA

Island of Minorca

Former capital of the island, this beautiful city, built around a small but welcoming harbour, has been granted the status of historic-artistic centre owing to the number and importance of its monuments.

The cathedral/basilica, **Ses Voltes**, **Es Bastió de sa Font**, which is today a museum, the "Plaza del Mercado" (market square) and the old quarter are truly charming areas.

Outstanding among the civic architecture are the numerous homes in the old quarter such as those of the **Saura**, **Olivar** and **Squella** families and others. It is possible to visit some of these homes. They demonstrate the importance that landowing nobility had in the city. Today, the majority of its 20,000 inhabitants earn their living directly from tourism. However, traditional industries such as shoes, fashion jewellery and agriculture still exist.

Ciutadella

The size of the picturesque harbour of Ciutadella was the main reason it lost its status as capital of the island, as its small size did not allow for the mooring of the fleets that arrived at the island.

Today, it is still the port for small cargo vessels from Majorca as well as many pleasure craft that moor alongside old fishing boats.

Its banks, especially on the South side, are lined with many restaurants and shops. The end of the port, or **Pla de Sant Joan** has a wide variety of bars and discos. This is the "in place" for the city's nightlife.

The port of Ciutadella is subject to a strange phenomenon, known as **Rissaga**. The coincidence of a series of atmospheric factors that occur during summer months provoke a sudden change in the sea level.

The water gradually withdraws only to return violently, flooding buildings and on occasions, such as in 1984, destroying the boats moored on its banks

The **Pla de Sant Joan** is surrounded by orchards that exemplify rural Minorcan architecture and during the fiestas, they become luxurious amphitheatres for watching the medieval games that take place there late on the 24th of June.

B *Es Pla de Sant Joan*

Sa Plaça de Es Borne, noted for its stately houses, offers views of the harbour from its viewpoint which is located above the old wall that surrounded the city.

The central obelisk was erected in memory of those courageous people who fought against the Turkish attack in1558.

C *Es Born*

The town hall occupies the old palace of the Muslim governor. The façade, of Byzantine style, was built in the XIX century by by the Catalan architect Josep Maria Sagnier. Especially interesting is its Gothic hall and its coffered woodwork. In the past it also housed a museum on the ground floor which has now been moved to the **Bastió de sa Font**.

D *Town Hall*

Ciutadella

E *The Cathedral*

The cathedral is the seat of the bishopric of Minorca. It was built on the site of the great mosque of Medina-Minurka and completed in 1362. The building is a clear example of Catalan Gothic, with a unique and very spacious nave, six chapels on each side and a pentagonal apse. It is one of the biggest cathedrals in the world with just one nave. Even though it has been subject to many attacks throughout its history (the last being during the civil war), its state of conservation is excellent.

A " must" to visit, as the ramifications of this picturesque road lead us into the old quarter of Ciutadella. Beneath its old arches one comes across all types of shops. Especially recommended are its patisseries where you can taste the famous Minorcan confectionery. Following the road towards the top, you will cross Plaça Nova that takes us to the old entrance of the city.

G *Es Molí*

F *Ses Voltes*

The mouth of the pretty harbour of Ciutadella is an excellent place to relax and observe the lazy Mediterranean sunset. On clear days neighbouring Majorca is visible.

1 *Mouth of the port*

2 *Sant Nicolau castle*

The castle of **Sant Nicolau**, named after a small chapel located nearby, formerly defended the entrance of Ciutadella harbour. The castle, as well as the square in which it is located, have recently been restored. It is possible to visit the castle during certain hours of the day.

3 *Sa Sectària*

Quarrying over the years in the **Sa Sectarèa** area has molded this coastal landscape that can be seen from the new seafront promenade that links the yacht club and **sa Platja Gran**.

The quarrying area's proximity to the coast facilitated shipment of the **marés** that was exported to Algeria for use by the Minorcan community who in past centuries emigrated there and who lived in Fort de L'Eau.

Ciutadella

The northern area is the steepest and most rocky area of the island and it offers beautiful and desolate landscapes. Shelters (barraques) were built to protect livestock from bad weather in an area where the **Tramuntana** wind vents its anger with particular violence. Virgin beaches and tall cliffs predominate in this area.

4 *Punta Nati*

As a result of the numerous shipwrecks that occurred in this area, the **Punta Nati** lighthouse was built. This is located at the most northerly end of the west coast of Ciutadella. This beautiful lighthouse can be visited via a narrow road that takes us to the base of the building. The surrounding land shows the devastating effects of the **Tramuntana**.

The architecture of the **Cala Morell** urbanization, made up mainly of houses, maintains a rustic line that fits in very well with the splendid landscapes that surround it. The land around the beach, except for the north face, is composed of a mixture of rocks that give way to the action of the sea. On the headland that encloses the beach, one can also see a stone figure that resembles an elephant.

5 *Cala Morell*

La Vall, with its wide expanse of pine trees and hundred year old oak trees, offers the two beautiful beaches of **Agaiarens**, namely **Sa Platja dels Tancats** and **Sa Platja de es Bot**. These are located in one of the most interesting nature areas and are recognized as being A.N.E.I (Natural Areas of Special Interest).

6 *La Vall*

Ciutadella

7 Cala en Carbó

Cala en Carbó, only accessible by sea or by a long walk through the woods, is one of the most solitary beaches in Minorca. Because of this certain birds, like the fish eagle, make their nests in the shelters of the cliffs of **Sa Punta Rotja**.

Es Macar d'Alfurinet, also known as **Es Pla de Mar**, is a truly spectacular place in which one finds a multitude of large lumps of rocks rounded by the action of sea swells. This is one of the few coves in Minorca with these characteristics. The **Muntanya Mala** cliff encloses the bay.

8 Es Pla de Mar

To reach this pretty cove, it is advisable to leave one's car at **Els Alocs** and continue on foot, following easily identifiable paths that lead one along the coast through beautiful landscapes.

Es Pilar is considered to be one of the most attractive natural beaches on the North coast. At the far west of the beach you will find a path that leads to **Es macar d'Alfurinet**.

9 El Pilar

The western area is the most built up area of Ciutadella although just going a little inland one discovers areas dedicated to agriculture. These areas have remained impassive to the passing of time and offer pretty rural scenes.

10 *Pont d'en Gil*

Nature's elements have formed fanciful shapes such as this arch which is near the **sa Torre del Ram** racecourse in the **Cales Piques** urbanization.
In the surrounding area you will find an underwater cave of great beauty that is often visited by scuba divers.

11 *Cales Piques*

Cales Piques is made up of two elongated and narrow coves. There is little sand. However, there is a rich rocky sea-floor that gives very varied colours to the waters. These range from emerald green to turquoise. Around these coves an important urbanization has developed.

At the end of a small gully we find the pretty **Cala en Forcat** where owing to its small area of sand and large number of visitors, platforms were built around it together with a series of communicating bridges which allow swimmers more enjoyment of this cove.

12 *Cala en Forcat*

This is a very attractive cove surrounded by cliffs. Looking at its sandy sea-floor from the platforms it gives the impression of being at the edge of a big swimming pool. The gully that culminates in the small beach contains examples of indigenous island flora including rosemary, different types of shrubs and small trees like savins.

13 *Cala en Brut*

Cala en Blanes was one of the first coves of Ciutadella to be urbanized. Its sea-floor is a combination of stones and sand. The picnic area, which is located at the rear of the beach and shaded by a small clump of palm trees, is interesting.

14 *Cala en Blanes*

Following the old road that links Ciutadella with **Cala en Blanes** that goes along the sea, we come across the tiny cove of **Sa Farola**. This is another option for those who live in the centre of the city to go for a quick dip!

15 *Cala de Sa Farola*

Ciutadella

Platja Petita and its neighbur **Platja Gran** are the closest beaches to the built-up area of Ciutadella and they have the advantage of being easily accessible. They are also known as **Cala De es Degollador** whose origin goes back to the Turkish invasion of Ciutadella. The islet of **sa Galera** encloses the bay.

16 *Sa Platja Petita*

Santandría and **Sa Caleta** are two small coves much loved by the locals. They still retain their charm even though they have been surrounded by urbanizations. In the cape that encloses these beaches we find **Es Castellar**, an old defence tower that today has been restored.

17 *Santandria and Sa Caleta*

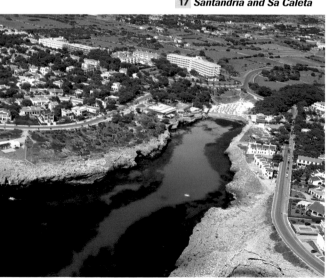

Despite being one of the oldest urbanizations, it has managed to preserve at least its vegetation. Here we find all sorts of buildings, from new hotels to pioneer apartment complexes. All, however, are surrounded by pinewood. Its advantage is being able to offer a wide range of services.

18 *Cala Blanca*

Ciutadella

19 *Sant Joan de Missa*

The chapel of **Sant Joan de Missa** is a typical example of rural Minorcan religious. architecture. It is easily visible on the side of the road that takes us towards the virgin beaches of the south. This beautiful building is well worth a visit.

20 *Cala en Bosc • Son Xoriguer*

One of the best planned urbanizations of the island, with many new infrastructures and services.

These two beaches offer the possibility of practising water-sports. At night there are a wide variety of restaurants that are located on the banks of a charming jetty known as El Lago.

21 *Son Saura*

Son Saura, made up of two sandy areas, is the start of a series of virgin beaches south of Ciutadella. For many, these are the best in the island. Surrounded by dense pinewoods, it offers brilliant white sands and crystal clear waters.

22 *Es Talaier*

Walking from **Son Saura** for a few minutes, you arrive at the beautiful **Cala de es Talaier**, which is much smaller but just as beautiful as its neighbours.

23 *Cala en Turqueta*

Following our trip from the western to the eastern virgin beaches, we come to **Cala en Turqueta**. The problem in reaching these beaches is due to difficult access because of the poor condition of the access roads. However, the effort in reaching these beaches is worthwhile as they have escaped tourist fever! These are ideal places in which to relax under the generous shade of their pine trees or in their clear waters.

Macarella and **Macarelleta**, surrounded by high cliffs, are the last beaches in this area. In **Macarella** there is the possibility of having a meal or a drink in the only beach bar of the area. **Macarelleta** is known as being one of the first nudist beaches in Minorca.

24 *Macarella • Macarelleta*

The quarrying of **marés**, a limestone used in building, has provoked the appearance of these amazing quarries that have been shaped by workers' saws of many generations. These quarries, located 1 km. away from Ciutadella, have been rehabilitated by the **Líthica** association and they host concerts and other social events. They can also be visited during the day.

26 *Naveta d'es Tudons*

The **Naveta de es Tudons**, located 3 km. from Ciutadella and accessible from the main road, is the most famous of the burial sites of the island. The navetes are communal burial sites of the Bronze age (1400 B.C.) as confirmed by the remains found in them.

27 *Taula Torretrencada*

The **taules** are the other most frequent archaeological sites on the island. Their origin and use are a cause of controversy among the experts. Some experts believe they are simple columns, while others believe they had a burial or sacrificial purpose.

28 *Taula Torre Llafuda*

In Minorca there are about 30 Taules left, but only a few still have the characteristic "T" shape.

This megalithic wall was a defence wall of the **Torre Llafuda** settlement, one of the most important settlements at the time.

28 *Defence wall of Torre Llafuda*

Ciutadella

The ancient settlements had large defensive walls, sometimes with underground tunnels for the defenders.

29 *Defence wall of Son Catlar*

It is believed that the **Cala Morell** caves were one of the first human settlements. Its natural caves were enlarged by man to satisfy the needs of a growing population. These caves can be easily visited from the nearby parking area.

Following this group of **Cala Morell** caves, we reach the interior of one of them, the **taula**, that acts as a column. This gives reason to the supporters of this hypothesis.

30 *Cala Morell caves*

The popular Minorcan fiestas are more than just tourist attractions. They are held in all municipalities and the black Minorcan horse is the central feature in all the fiestas. The most famous fiesta of all is that of Sant Joan de Ciutadella.

The fiestas of Sant Joan start on the Sunday prior to June 23rd which is called **Es Diumenge de es Be**. The fiestas continue on the 23th and 24th, the days of the main fiesta. During these days the streets are covered with sand and decked out with lights as though people would like to make the summer solstice last longer. The fiestas are subject to strict protocols, whose origins are lost in the mists of time, and are known and respected by the locals who wait for the fiestas with unusual impatience.

The most important participants of the fiesta are the **Caixers** who make up the Brotherhood Committee of **Sant Joan**. They watch over the perfect proceedings of the fiestas. Amongst these we recognize the **Caixer Fadrí** (the bachelor) who carries the flag of the Maltese cross, the **Menestral** (the craftsman), the **Caixer Casat** (the married man), two **Caixers Pagesos** (country men) and above everyone else, the **Caixer Senyor**, chosen twice a year from the members of the old nobility. He is the leader of the **Caixers** Committee. The rest of the cavalcade that parades in the **Caragols** is made up of **Cavallers** or riders who come

from the countryside. Other participants include **Sa Capellana**, a rider who belongs to the clergy (who comes last in the group) and **Sa Somareta**, a donkey ridden by **Es Fabioler** who plays his **Fabiol** (a type of small flute) and marks the rhythm of the festivities. Especially colourful are the equestrian games that take place in **Es pla de Sant Joan** at the end of the harbour on the afternoon of the 24th. Among these the game of **s'Ensortilla** stands out. Here a rider armed with a lance has to lance some small rings that hang from a rope whilst in full gallop. Then comes the game of **Ses Carotes** where some wooden shields are broken by the riders, much to the rejoicing of the spectators who rush forward towards the fragments in order to grab a piece as a souvenir of the fiestas. To mark the end of these games, there is the game of **Correr Abraçats**. This consists of riders in pairs embracing each other in full gallop along the small path made by the human tide of people embracing each other.

with lemonade is the typical fiesta drink and it is consumed in great quantities! Another essential element are hazelnuts. Tons of these cover the ground after being thrown into the air as a symbol of joy. Fireworks in the early hours of the 25th mark the end of the fiestas, that are unforgettable for those who have never been to the fiestas before.

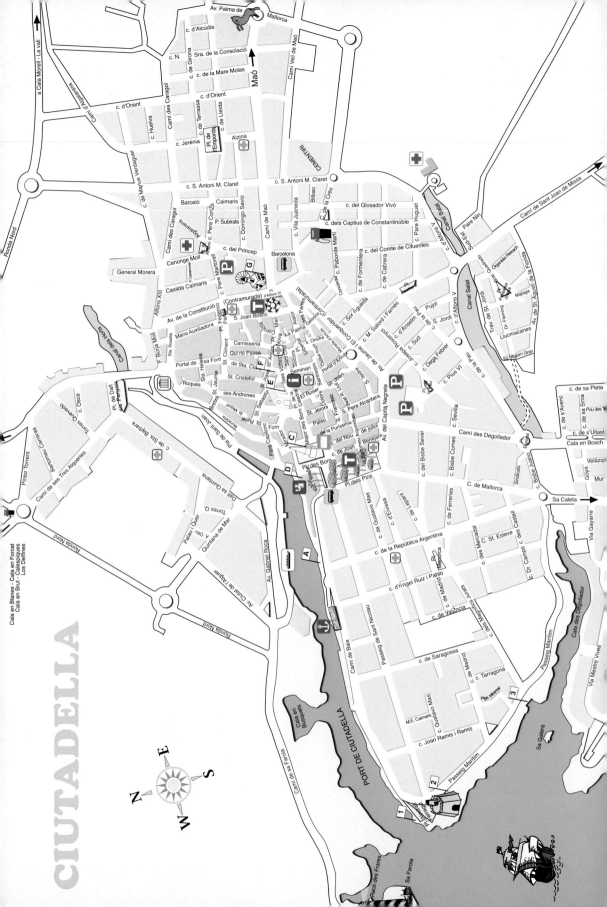

This town is situated in an area surrounded by hills and it is famous for its shoe making and furniture making industry. It has a population of about 5,000. In its old quarter there are buildings of historic interest such as the church of **Sant Bartomeu**. There are also enchanting spots, such as the **Carrer de sa Font**, that contrast with the growth that the town has experienced in recent years that has resulted in the expansion of the industrial estate. Tourism in the area is concentrated in the **Cala Galdana** beach which is about 8 km. from the town.

TOWN CENTRE

NORTHERN AREA

SOUTHERN AREA

BARRANC D'ALGENDAR

ARCHAEOLOGICAL AREA

Island of Minorca

B *Esglèsia de Sant Bartomeu*

In this page we can see different aspects of the town. The top page shows a panoramic view of Ferreries taken from the **s'Enclusa** mountain that is the site of a former American military base at its top.

In the other two pictures, we can see the church of **Sant Bartomeu** and the town's main square.

A *Plaça d'Espanya*

Ferreries TOWN CENTRE

Being surrounded by small hills, the inhabitants of Ferreries have taken advantage of this for farming by building small terraces which are very useful in stemming the flow of torrential rainwater.

Despite the rural aspect the town presents, Ferreries has an important shoe-making industry and in the industrial estate there is one of the most renown factories on a national level.

Climbing to the top of any of the surrounding hills offers interesting views like this one in which we can see the stream that crosses the town.

Ferreries

The northern area, riddled with hills, is the least inhabited in the municipality. The little white houses are dotted around a very green landscape that has a very rich ornithological wealth.

The ruins of **Santa Águeda** castle, located a few kilometres from the town, are traces of the Arab domination of the island.
A visit on foot is recommended from its base via a cobbled path that takes one to the top and the ruins and at the same time enjoying the beautiful landscape.

1 *Santa Águeda castle*

The steep cliffs in the northern area conceal little treasures such as **Cala en Calderer** that, like most of these coves, is not easily accessible.

2 *Cala en Calderer*

One of the shelters in the north that is most frequented by the locals is **Els Alocs**. Here one finds a large number of huts that are used mainly at weekends. Easily accessible apart from the last stretch.

3 *Els Alocs*

4 Barranc d'Algendar

In the southern area we find numerous gullies that are home to a large part of the indigenous flora and fauna of Minorca. The photograph shows the end of the **d'Algendar** gully.

From Ferreries we take the turning that leads to **Cala Mitjana**, its little sister **Cala Mitjaneta** and the beautiful cove of **Cala Galdana**. The three beaches are very beautiful and they are surrounded by pine trees that offer a space in which to relax after having enjoyed their crystal clear waters.

5 *Cala Mitjaneta*

Cala Mitjana and **Cala Galdana** reflect the two faces of tourism. Whilst the former retains its virgin state, being a lure for tourism, the latter has been heavily built up and offers a wide variety of services.

6 *Cala Mitjana*

Although there are a few large hotels bordering the beach, this beach continues to be considered one of the most beautiful on the island. Especially recommended are its two viewpoints that offer enchanting views of not only the end of the **d'Algendar** stream but also the spectacular cliffs that enclose the bay.

7 *Cala Galdana*

⁴ BARRANC D'ALGENDAR

This, together with **s'Albufera de es Grau**, is one of the spots of great natural interest. A wide variety of birds find ideal nesting places in its high faces. The only continuous stream on the island makes possible a large population of reptiles and amphibians, such as the harmless water snake and various types of frog.

8 *The son Fideu gully*

9 *Son Mercer*

A settlement that boasts one of the most ancient non-burial navetes. This is perhaps the richest archaeological site of Ferreries and it is reached by a tortuous cobbled path through two **llocs**. The hardships of the journey are compensated by beautiful views of the **Son Fideu** gully.

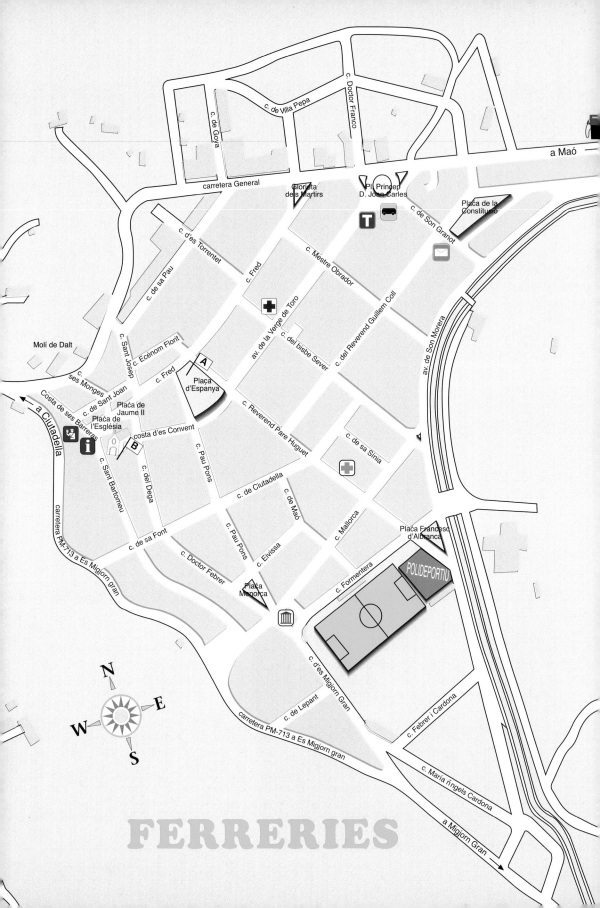

This picturesque small town of small white houses is situated in the centre of the island. The landscape of green fields that surround it is typically rural. Next to the town is the **Monte Toro** mountain that seems higher than it is because Es Mercadal is the town with the lowest height above sea level on the island.

This small town is famous for its confectionary and in its patisseries we can buy macaroons and **carquinyols**, two of the most popular specialities. Es Mercadal is an area rich in springs and there is the only bottling plant for Minorcan water located here.

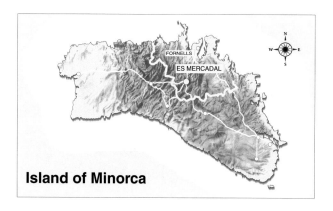

Island of Minorca

Es Mercadal

As traces of a past tied to agriculture, the town still has a few relics such as the mill in a perfect state of preservation or this well that adorns one of its streets.

A *Molí des Racó*

Es **Molí de es Racó**, easily recognizable on the side of the main road, houses a restaurant where you can taste some of the specialities of typical Minorcan cuisine whilst contemplating the Monte Toro mountain.

Cobbled streets, whitewashed walls. Walking through the old streets of Es Mercadal gives one the impression that time has stood still.

Like Ferreries, Es Mercadal also has a stream through it that channels torrential rainwater that falls in spring and autumn.

Es Mercadal

1 *Penya de s'Indi*

Leaving Es Mercadal and going towards Maó we find another quirk of nature. Years of erosion have created a figure that with a little imagination appears to be the head of a Red Indian chief. There is a viewpoint that allows a more detailed observation of this natural sculpture.

A constant feature of the interior landscape of Minorca is the **paret seca** that separates the green pasture fields and the large number of livestock of the island.

Many of the farmhouses had their own mill. The prickly pears, very much in evidence in the northern area, are another trick in holding back the inclement **Tramuntana**.

Es Mercadal

Another must for any self-respecting tourist. The viewpoints are a gift to the eyes and there are excellent spots for taking panoramic photographs of the island. It is also very interesting to visit the small church which is a place of worship dedicated to the patron saint of Minorca. It is attached to a Franciscan convent. To reach the church, you cross a pretty inner patio where there is a bar that has marvellous views and a small souvenir shop.

MONTE TORO

Monte Toro

The ascent from Es Mercadal to the mountain can also be made on foot on an excursion of some 3 km., that allows you to view the landscape whilst walking to the top. During the ascent you can see the old slate quarries whose material was widely used in the past for building.

Es Mercadal

Easily distinguishable from the southern coves by their reddish sand, the beaches in the north combine clear waters with beautiful landscapes. In some, like **Caballería** or **Pilar**, there are small hills of clayey earth that many swimmers like to apply to their skin.

3 *Cavalleria*

This is the most easily accessible beach in this area. It has a car park just a few metres from the sand. Its sand is a little coarser than its neighbours as it is mixed with fine gravel. Next to the car park is a small wetland area that is inhabited by marsh birds.

4 *Binimel.là*

The large reefs that seem to guard **Cala Pregonda** and **Cala Pregondó** turn them into an excellent haven in the middle of the rough north coast. Getting there takes some 15 minutes from nearby **Binimel.lá**.

5 *Cala Pregonda • Pregondó*

In the environs of **Cap de Cavalleria**, you find the small hidden coves of **Cala Torta**. Facing totally north, they are another spot to discover in the **Tramuntana** of es Mercadal.

6 *Cala Torta*

Between **Cala Torta** and **Sa Nitja** there are archaeological remains of what was one of the first settlements that the Roman conquerors established on the island.

7 *Sa Nitja*

The jetty of **Sa Nitja** is one of the few privileged places where boats can rest up in calm waters. It is used by many fishermen during the lobster fishing season.

8 *Sa Nitja*

Es Mercadal

Arenal de Son Saura, better known as **Son Parc**, is one of the few beaches in this area that has very fine white sand. A small strip of dunes and a dense pinewood complete the landscape. The urbanization boasts the only golf-club on the island.

9 *Arenal de Son Saura (Son Parc)*

The beach is the most perfect shell-shape cove in Minorca and one of the longest. Notwithstanding the many hotels that surround it, it offers plenty of free space on its sands.

10 *Arenal de en Castell*

This small fishing village with its own small cove is one of the favourite spots for anglers.

11 *Na Macaret*

Es Mercadal

11 *Addaia • Na Macaret • Cala Molí*

Port d'Addaia is one of the favourite havens for mooring boats. Its long and narrow inlet provides a marina sheltered by **sa Illa de ses Mones**.

12 *Port d'Addaia*

Cala Molí is another of the many inlets found around **Addaia**. Its coast is surrounded by dense marshes that provide shelter for the typical birds of this area

13 *Cala Moli*

14 *Cap de Cavalleria*

Cap de Cavalleria is the most northerly point in Minorca. It forms a small peninsula that ends in a crag of tall cliffs, especially in the Levant zone. On the western side the height drops gradually until it reaches the coast and whose end seems to point out the **Illa dels Porros**. On its northern side and leaning out to the sea is one of the most important lighthouses on the island.

Sheltered in the interior of
the bay of the same name,
you find the growing village of
Fornells. It is a village well known
for the quality of its restaurants
and for the many boating and
sailing facilities. At the end
of the bay there are remains
of pools which used
to be used for salt extraction.

After having tasted the typical "caldereta de langosta" you can take a relaxing walk along the small but well looked after promenade that is lined with palm trees. At dusk you can see the return of small fishing boats after a long day at sea.

C *Fornells promenade*

Fornells castle, recently restored, is one of the places recommended for a visit. Built by the British near the site of the old fort of **St. Antoni**, its walls, that are full of history, lean out towards the sea.

15 *Fornells castle*

The coasts of this small interior sea are dotted with tiny coves from which you can observe maritime traffic or the whimsical flight of seagulls. The shortest way of reaching the coves is by sea because of the difficulties involved in reaching them by land.

16 *The bay of Fornells*

Es Mercadal

17 *Platges de Fornells - Cala Tirant*

In **Cala Tirant**, in its eastern area, you will find what is perhaps the largest urbanization of the area. At the rear of the beach there is a small wetland area surrounded by tamarind.

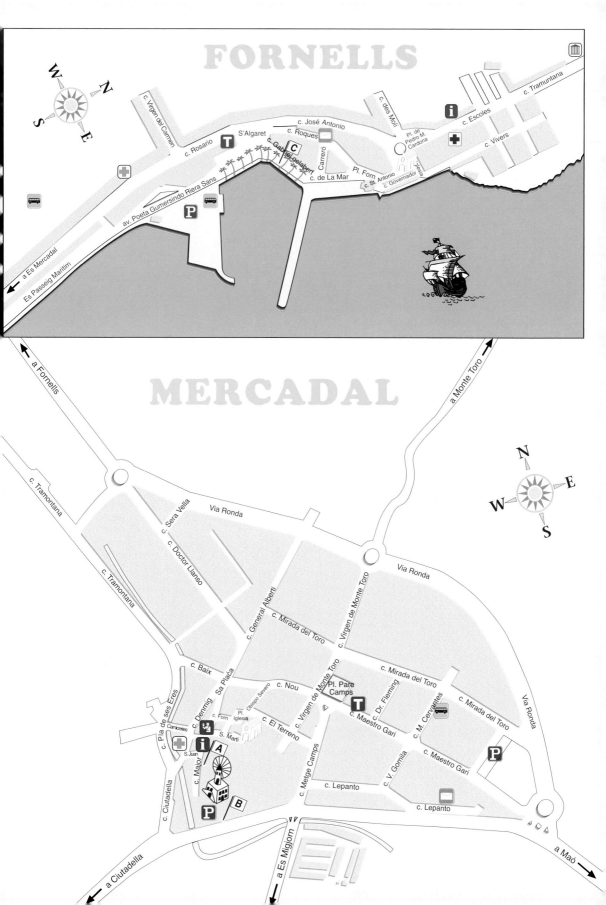

FORNELLS

W N
S E

c. Tramuntana

c. Virgen del Carmen

c. Rosario

S'Algaret

c. José Antonio
c. Roques

c. des Moll

c. Escoles

c. Vivers

c. Gabriel gelabert

Carreró

Pl. de
Pedro M.
Cardona

c. de La Mar

Pl. Forn

c. St. Antonio

c. Governador

av. Poeta Gumersindo Riera Sans

a Es Mercadal

Es Passeig Marítim

MERCADAL

a Fornells

a Monte Toro

N
W E
S

c. Tramontana

Sera Vella

Via Ronda

c. Doctor Llanso

c. Tramontana

Via Ronda

c. General Alberti

c. Mirada del Toro

c. Virgen de Monte Toro

Via Ronda

c. Baix

c. Mirada del Toro

c. Nou

Sa Plaça

c. Dentmig

Carriones

c. Pla de ses Eres

c. Forn

Pl.
Iglesia

Obispo Severo

S. Marti

S. Juan

c. Major

A

c. Virgen de Monte Toro

Pl. Pare
Camps

T

c. Dr. Fleming

c. M. Cervantes

c. Mirada del Toro

c. El Terreno

c. Maestro Gari

c. Maestro Gari

B

c. Metge Camps

c. V. Gomila

c. Ciutadella

c. Lepanto

c. Lepanto

a Ciutadella

a Es Migjorn

a Maó

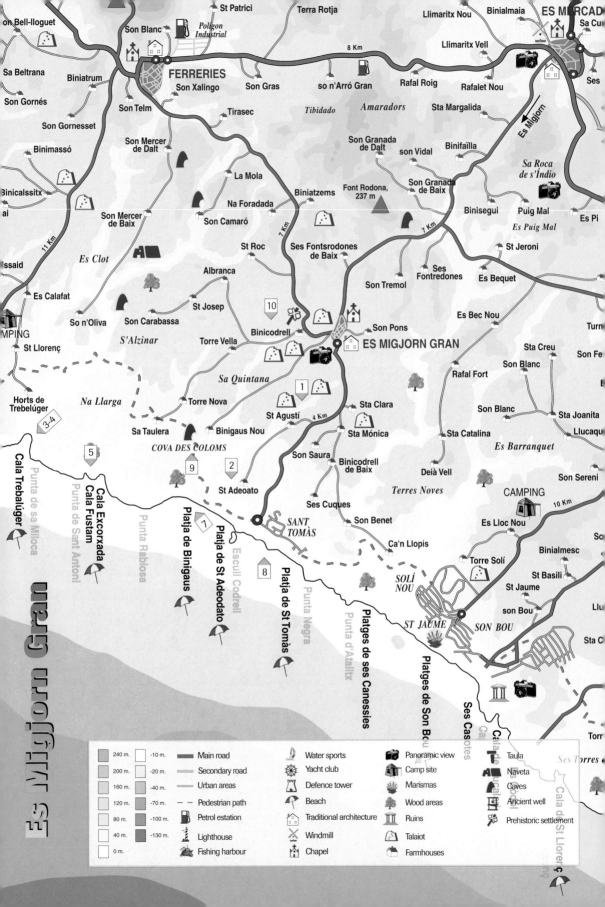

TOWN CENTRE
SOUTHERN AREA
COVA DE ES COLOMS
ARCHAEOLOGICAL AREAS

Island of Minorca

The small town of De's Migjorn Gran was initially a group of settlements during the second half of the XVIIIth century during the second British domination of Minorca.

It is the youngest municipality on the island and it broke away from Es Mercadal of which it formed part in 1989. Its layout, similar to others in Minorca, has its origin around a church, namely **Sant Cristòfol**, around which this tranquil town extended to a population of about 3,000.

The access roads to Migjorn from Ferreries and Es Mercadal are very pretty as they are surrounded by a dense pinewood. The roads, however, can be somewhat winding. Like its neighbour, Ferreries, it also has some of the characteristic gullies of the southern area, like **Binigaus** where the largest cave is situated (**sa Cova des Coloms**).

Es Migjorn Gran

On this page we can see different aspects of this small and enchanting town. Its adjoining land is used for cultivation. It is divided into small orchards that are separated by **paret seca** (dry stone walls). We can also see the much cared for church of **Sant Cristòfol** and one of its quiet streets.

A *The church of Sant Cristòfol*

In the town's surrounding area, there are farmhouses of typical rural Minorcan architecture, built of **marés**. On their land one finds indigenous trees, such as fig trees, together with others that were imported, like palms.

A visit to the large number of orchards on the outskirts of this town confirm the importance that agriculture has played in this municipality. The hills, as in Ferreries, have been converted into small terraces.

To reach the **lloc de Binigaus** and the gully of the same name, one must take this pretty road that is protected by old pine trees.

1 *Camí de Binicodrell*

Es Migjorn Gran

2 *The Binigaus gully*

The area south of Migjorn has beautiful gullies and wide beaches. The photo shows a well, hewn from the rock, that is located in the **Binigaus** gully.

3 *The Trebalúger gully*

4 *Trebalúger*

Following the **sa Cova** or **son Fideu** gully, we reach **Trebalúger** beach. The soil that makes up these gullies is very fertile and the stream that crosses them distributes water in abundance. This allows the cultivation of all types of produce from the orchards. The fine sand of the beach forms a barrier that encloses the stream that during the dry season remains stagnant. The **Punta de sa Miloca** encloses this beach, which is one of the least frequented of the area.

5 *Cala Fustam • Cala Escorxada*

Following an easterly direction, we find the small coves of **Cala Fustam** and **Escorxada**, separated some 400 metres by the **Sant Antoni** point. The extensive natural area that surrounds them, made up of pine trees that reach the cliffs, is of great importance.

7 *Binigaus*

Binigaus, **San Adeodato** and **Santo Tomás**, are three beaches that are practically joined together. Tourism and services are concentrated in this area. In the first of these beaches the cliffs descend into the sand. It is the least used, and it is quite common to come across nudist sunbathing on its small strip of beach.

8 *San Adeodato • Sant Tomàs*

At the other two beaches in the area, separated by the **Codrell** islet, there are hotels situated on the front line of the sea and a series of tourist facilities such as supermarkets, bars and even a discos. The second line of the urbanization is made up of villas.

Es Migjorn Gran

9 | COVA DE ES COLOMS

To reach the spectacular **Cova de es Coloms**, the largest cave on the island, you have to head towards the **Binigaus** estate where, from one of the gully walls of the same name, you can admire this enormous cave. Owing to its size (approx. 24 metres high by 11 metres long and 15 metres wide) it is also known as **sa Catedral** (the cathedral). Numerous talayotic era remains were found in its interior.

10 *Talaiots de Binicodrell*

Following the path that leads to the **Binigaus** gully, you can see from the same edge the archaeological site of Bini Codrell in which there are large **talaiots**. One of these is empty and it is possible to enter it.

The **Talaiots** were used as signal towers and bonfires were lit on their roofs to warn of danger of possible invaders. From the roof of one of these buildings at least two others were visible which resulted in communications network that extended all over the island. One of the first names given to Minorca was "Nura" that means "fire" in Phoenician, a reference to the bonfires that alerted the presence of unknown boats on the coast.

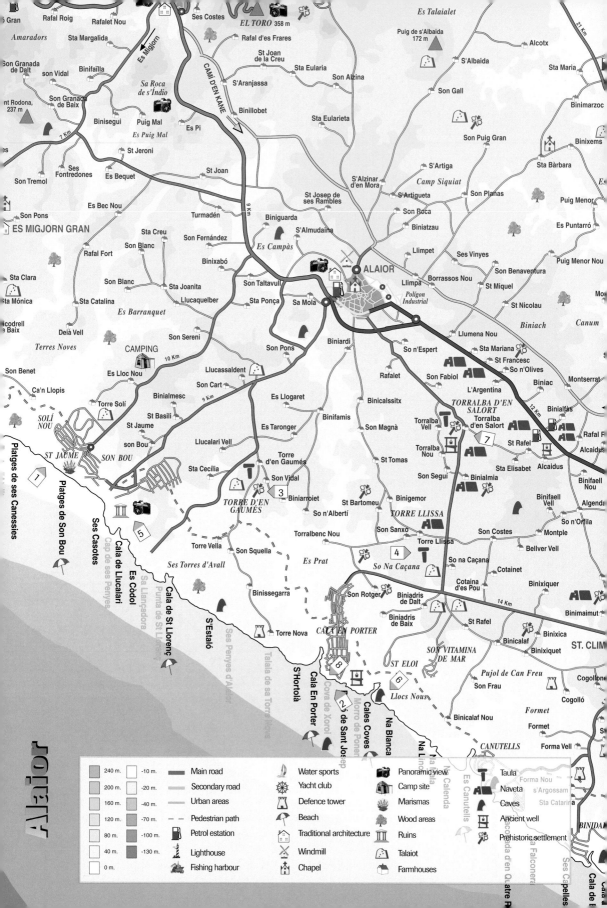

TOWN CENTRE
SOUTHERN AREA
ARCHAEOLOGICAL AREA
CALAS COVES
TAULA DE TORRALBA
COVA DE EN XOROI

Island of Minorca

Alaior, founded by the Catalan king Jaime II, is the third town in Minorca in terms of population with some 9,000 inhabitants.

The view of the town with its white houses climbing up a gentle hill, is one of the most beautiful of Minorca. It hides a layout of very irregular streets in which you can find some interesting noble houses such as **Can Salort**.

Its economy is based on industry such as its important shoe factories and the making of cheese which is sold as "Queso Mahón Menorca". This town was a pioneer in the ice-cream industry and it is the cradle of the well known La Menorquina brand, that to-day is owned by a company outside the island.

The archaeological wealth on its outskirts is very important and includes the prehistoric settlements of **Torre de Gaumés** and **Torralba de Salord** as well as the paleo-cristian basilica located near **Son Bou** beach. **Son Bou** together with **Cala en Porter** are the tourist centres of this area.

Alaior

A *Bell tower of Santa Eulalia*

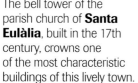

The bell tower of the parish church of **Santa Eulàlia**, built in the 17th century, crowns one of the most characteristic buildings of this lively town.

B *The Sant Diego cloister*

The old cloister of the church of San Diego, known to the Minorcans as **Es Pati de sa Lluna** dates from the 17th century and a visit is recommended.

B *Es Pati de sa Lluna*

The town of Alaior was built on the site of an old Muslim settlement called Ihalor. This town has always been a staging post between Ciutadella and Maó.

In these photographs we can see different aspects of the church of **Santa Eulàlia** which is one of the reference points of the city. Its facade has a central rose window and at each end there are turrets that resemble minarets.

Alaior

The southern area of Alaior is known for its large number of prehistoric remains and for having the longest stretch of sand in Minorca, namely the beach of **Son Bou.**

1 Son Bou

The sandy area of **Son Bou** which is reached by passing under an arch hewn out of stone, is the longest beach in Minorca of nearly 4 km. in length. Near the beach there are a large number of tourist services, typical of a large urbanization. Following the beach, we come to some wetlands that are in a quite good state of conservation. They are the second most important wetland area of Minorca.

2 Cala en Porter

Cala en Porter is the second most important urbanization in this area. Here we find curious houses that appear to hang from the walls of its tall cliffs. The beach is found at the mouth of the gully and there is a wetland area at the end of the gully. Going through the streets of the urbanization, we reach the legendary **Cova de en Xoroi**.

Alaior

3 *Torre d'en Gaumés*

Following a turning off the road towards **Son Bou**, we reach the prehistoric settlement of **Torre de en Gaumes**. In this large settlement of some 62,000 sq. metres, we find all sorts of archaeological remains. Three **talaiots** dominate the area. At the base of these **talaiots** there is an enclosure for a taula where a statuette of the Egyptian god Imhotep was found, among other remains. Looking around the area we can see remains of defensive walls, water tanks excavated in the rock, caves etc… A little further away there is the megalithic tomb of **ses Roques Llises** and the hypostyle hall of **sa Comerma de sa Garita**.

4 *Torre Llisa*

Taking the Alaior to **Cala en Porter** road you find the ruins of the **Torre Llisa** settlement. Though not as famous as **Torre de en Gaumes** it is worth visiting. This settlement has two large **talaiots** and various enclosure walls that indicate the former presence of **taules** that supported the tops of these structures.

5 *Basilica paleo-cristiana de Son Bou*

These remains of a paleo-Christian basilica are located at the eastern end of the **Son Bou** beach, next to the sea and they can be easily visited. Built in the 5th century, it is perhaps the most famous basilica on the island. Outstanding is its large four leaf clover shaped baptismal font. Some caves can be found near these remains.

Alaior

6 *Cales Coves*

Taking a dirt road in the **Son Vitamina** urbanization, you reach Cales Coves which is made up of two small coves that are sheltered by tall cliffs. Many small boats choose these waters to anchor. Most outstanding here are the large number of caves, more than one hundred, that were bored in the walls of their gullies. These caves are the most important prehistorical necropolis in the Balearic Islands. There are two groups of caves. One group, the oldest, (8th and 9th century B.C.) is made up of small caves with rounded entrances, whilst the second group, (6th century B.C. to the Roman era), is made up of bigger caves with niches in their interiors. Some of these caves were lived in until recently by old hippies who were evicted in order to preserve this important site.

7 *Torralba d'en Salord*

In the settlement of **Torralba de en Salord** you will find the most emblematic taula in Minorca. It is one of the largest, being 3 metres high and 2.5 metres wide. At the base of its vertical stone that weighs some 16 tons, various important remains were discovered including some statuettes, one representing a bull and a horse.

8 COVA DE EN XOROI

From the **Cala en Porter** urbanization we can reach **Cova de en Xoroi**, a spectacular natural cave in the high cliff walls. This cave, that is a lively disco during summer nights, can be visited during the day. A small entrance fee is charged. On the wall of the bar area you can read one of the oldest and most beautiful legends of Minorca, that of the Moor **Xoroi**.

ALAIOR

Maó, capital of Minorca, has been the administrative centre of the island since the 18th century. It is also the public health, military and communications centre, thanks to its splendid port and its nearby airport. Its population of some 23,000 inhabitants is mainly involved in industry and trade. The best way of visiting the city is on foot, leaving your car at the **Plaça de s'Esplanada** or Plaza Miranda underground car-parks or in **sa Sinia de es Cuc** (free). Walking along the most central streets such as ses Moreres, **Costa de sa Plaça**, **Carrer Nou**, **s'Arravaleta** etc., one realizes the British influence on the civic architecture of Maó. Examples of this influence are the many boinders (bow-windows) and sash-windows.

The city has two interesting parks. One is **Es Freginal** and the other is the new Rubio i Tuduri park where many species of indigenous plants can be found. The old town-centre was walled-in centuries ago. The only remains of this wall can be found at **Es Pont de Sant Roc**. Interesting buildings include the churches or **Sant Francesc**, **el Carme** and **Santa Maria**. The town-hall and the Teatro Principal (the theatre) are also interesting. Amongst the civic architecture one comes across some modernist style houses strolling around the streets.

TOWN CENTRE

NORTHERN AREA

ALBUFERA DE ES GRAU

ILLA DE EN COLOM

LA MOLA - EL LLATZAREL

ARCHAEOLOGICAL AREAS

SANT CLIMENT - SOUTHERN AREA

Island of Minorca

A *Port de Maó*

The great port of Maó, of about 6 kms. in length and with a width that varies from 240 to 1,200 metres, has always been a favourite anchorage point for large vessels. The fleets of days gone by that used to moor on its banks have been substituted by modern transatlantic cruisers that visit the port almost daily during the summer. There were five islets in the mouth of the port. To-day, one can only see three. These are the **Illa del Rei**, where Alfonso III landed to conquer the island, the **Illa de sa Quarantena** and **la Illa del Llatzaret**. Each islet has its own history.

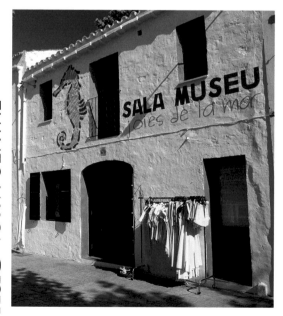

The southern bank of the port offers a wide variety of tourist services. Summer nights are the liveliest! Here there are may restaurants, bars and even a new casino where gamblers can try their luck!

To reach the port from the town, we recommend using the pretty steps called **ses Voltes** that are surrounded by fragrant gardens. From here you can see the **Can Mir** building, one of the best examples of modernist architecture in Maó.

B *Ses Voltes*

Maó

C *Carme church*

D *Plaça Reial*

Maó

D *Santa Maria*

The church of **Santa Maria** is the largest of its kind in Maó. Built in the 18th century, as were many other buildings in the town, this church has only one very high nave with vaults topped by four groins. The most outstanding feature of this church is its large organ which is some 15 metres tall and 8 metres wide. Its four keyboards play 3,006 pipes, 197 of them made out of wood. In the right hands they give off a great sound quality. In summer, concerts are usually held and these are known as "Matins a l'Orgue".

F *Sa Sala*

Maó town-hall, also known as **Sa Sala**, is one of the city`s most characteristic buildings. Also built in the 18th century, its neo-classical façade still carries the clock that the British governor, Richard Kane, brought to Minorca. A part of the town-hall is open to the public in which one can admire some old portraits. In its elegant assembly hall there are portraits of the town's distinguished citizens. Following the narrow street on the side of the façade, you reach **Plaça de la Conquesta** in which there is a statue of Alfonso III.

1 *Es Portixol*

The lands of northern Maó were formed in the Palaeozoic period and thus are one of the oldest in the Balearics. The land, which is a dark colour, is made up of slate and quartz sandstone and it is clearly visible in the cut down cliffs.

From the road that leads you to the **Favàritx** or **Capifort** lighthouse, you can reach the small pot-shaped cove of **es Portixol** which has one of the few beaches of greyish sand in Minorca. Being totally north facing, it is frequently subjected to winter storms.

1 *Cala de es Portixol*

The **Favàritx** lighthouse is one of the most important in Minorca. The cut down slate of its land only allows the growth of small plants and thus many liken it to a lunar landscape. When a severe **Tramuntana** blows it really is spectacular here as white sea-foam and the black rock meet.

2 *Cap de Favàritx*

On the opposite side of **Es Portixol** and sheltered by the small Favaritx peninsula you will find **Cala Presili**. Its whitish sand stands out very strongly as it is framed in an even lighter blue colour of its waters.

3 *Cala Presili*

5 *Sa Mesquida*

A mere 5 kms. away from Maó is **Cala Mesquida**, one of the favourite beaches for people who live in Maó and you park your car practically on the sand. The beach is flanked on one side by the crag of **Es Pa Gros** and on the other side by a promontory on which there is an old defence tower.

4 *Sa Mesquida*

Before reaching the beach there is a small urbanization of houses whose old architecture leads us to deduce that this tourist enclave was founded many years ago. It is curious to see how even small islets have become humanized!

6 Albufera d'Es Grau

The **Es Grau** lagoon is the first and only nature reserve in Minorca and it is the nucleus of the Biosphere Reserve, owing to its special characteristics and state of conservation. The protected area is of approximately 1,800 hectares. 70 of these hectares are under water. The lagoon has a narrow and elongated shape and it is joined to the sea by **Sa Gola**, a small channel that runs near the urbanization of **Es Grau**. Another old urbanization of houses is Shangri-La, which is located at its rear part. The land was formed in the carboniferous period and it is home to a large and wide number of ornithological species, including herons, bald-coots, moorhens and some marine birds of prey. During the migratory months this nature reserve is especially busy as it is a resting point between Europe and Africa. In its briny waters eels, sea bass and a species of turtle are quite common. There is an information point near **sa Gola**.

ALBUFERA DE ES GRAU **Maó**

7 Illa d'En Colom

The island of **en Colom** also belongs to the nucleus of the biosphere reserve. It is the largest islet of the island and measures some 60 hectares. In order to visit it, you need to take a boat that leaves from **Es Grau** and reaches the shore where there are two small coves. On the islet there are remains of an early Christian basilica as well as a quarantine building that was used by the Spaniards and the English in the 18th century. As far as fauna is concerned, there exists here an endemic subspecies of **sargantana** (lizard) which is also found on other islets.

8 *La Mola*

Following the north road of the port of Maó, you reach the military peninsula of **La Mola**, located between the very narrow isthmus of **els Freus** and the **Punta de s'Esperó**. In the past this crag was the main military nucleus of Minorca and it had various fortifications such as Isabel II, that defended the mouth of the port with numerous artillery pieces. Its ruined walls bear witness to numerous executions, the last being during the civil war. The military installations, now in disuse, were used as a military prison until 1968. There is a military museum within that can be visited by prior appointment by calling the military administration.

9 *Llatzaret*

La **Illa del Llatzaret** is the biggest islet in the port of Maó. In 1900 the small isthmus that connected it to the land was destroyed. The main building was built with materials that came from the demolition of **Sant Felip** castle. El Llatzaret (quarantine building) was in use until 1917 and it was an obligatory stopping point for ships heading towards the peninsula. These ships needed to be in quarantine for a certain time in order to be given an epidemic-free certification. The most interesting part of the islet is its cemetery , situated at the rear of the island, which has a Catholic and Protestant section. In one of the buildings there is a medical museum with genuine equipment of the time.

10 Taula de Trepucó

ARCHAEOLOGICAL AREAS

The Maó area, like the rest of the island, has important archaeological sites. Following the cemetery road for about 2 kms. from the city, you reach the enormous Taula de **Trepucó** that is located in an area where you also come across a **talaiot** and other remains.

11 *Taula de Talatí de Dalt*

Following the Maó to Ciutadella road and passing the airport turning, you change direction for access to **Talatí de Dalt**. The taula we find in this enclosure is unusual insofar as it is reinforced by a second leaning column. This area also has a talaiot. However, the most outstanding points are its semi-subterranean hypostyle halls that are to be found on an inclination of the land.

12 *Navetes de Rafal Rubí*

Going towards Ciutadella and at approximately 500 metres before the petrol station, there is a turning towards the **Navetes** of **Rafal Rubí**. There are funeral navetes situated in a field and there are similarities with the Naveta de **Es Tudons** in Ciutadella, although its construction is slightly less refined.

13 *Sant Climent*

Leaving Maó and heading towards **Cala en Porter**, you reach the small village of Sant Climent which is administered by Maó Town Council. The most outstanding building of the village is the small parish church. It has pointed archivolts and a central rose-window . This church is one of the most modern emblematic churches, having been built in the 19th century . Also noticeable in Sant Climent are the pubs to be found anywhere in Britain. Sant Climent has quite a large British colony who are jazz lovers and jazz concerts are regularly held here, especially during the summer, twice a week. Close to the village there are ruins of an early Christian basilica in **Fomás de Torelló** that has an extraordinary mosaic. Leaving the village in a southerly direction you reach the beaches south of Maó.

SANT CLIMENT **Maó**

14 *Es Canutells*

The south part of Maó has, more than any other place, typical Minorcan rural architecture. This is an area with red painted facades dotted around. The area also has some beaches that have gullies, such as **Es Canutells**.

On a slope in the land surrounded by typical Minorcan scrub-land, you will find the small hidden cove of **Biniparratx**, the least used in the area. There is a camping area nearby that is used in the summer by groups of youngsters.

15 *Biniparratx*

The small **Binidalí** is a growing urbanization, mainly made up of luxury holiday homes. The beach is to be found at the end of a small gully, hidden by some cliffs.

16 *Binidalí*

Es Canutells, located at the end of a gully, is a slightly wider beach than its neighbours. Although it is surrounded by a large urbanization, especially at its most easterly part, it is still used by a small group of fishermen and fishing boats who refuse to abandon their trade and thus lend it a typical air of the place.

17 *Es Canutells*

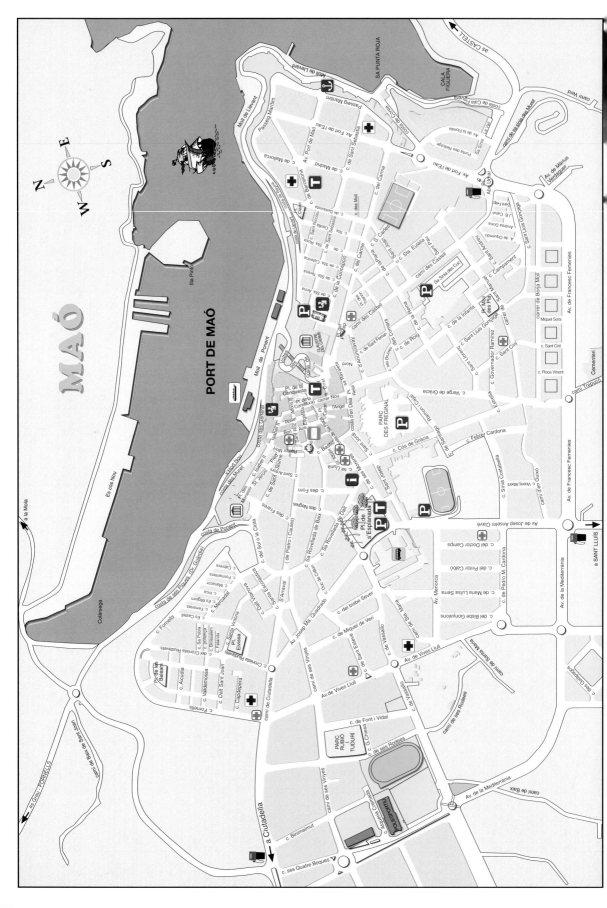

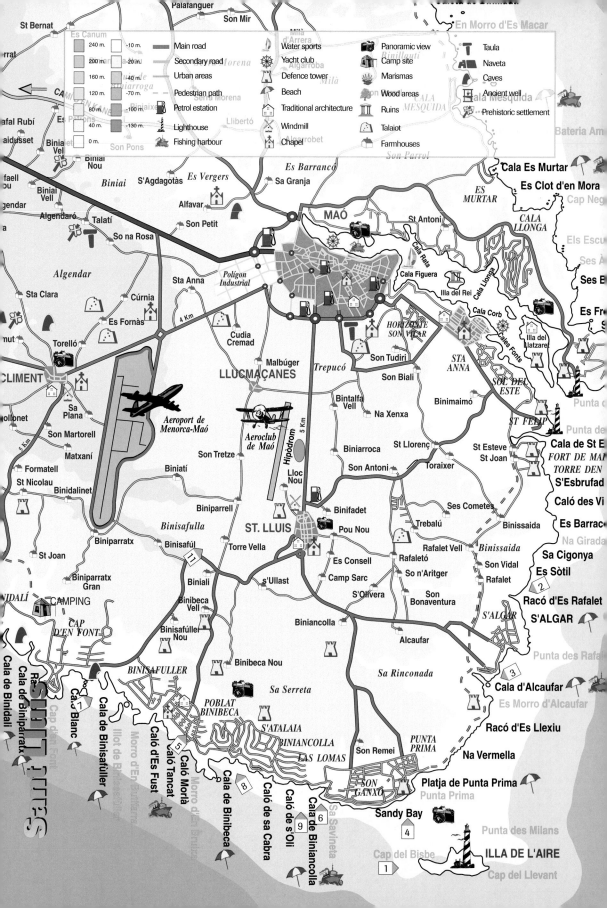

A *Molí de Dalt*

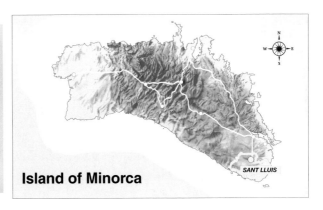

Island of Minorca

SANT LLUIS

This small town is different from other municipalities in that it was founded by the French during their short period of domination of Minorca (1756-1763). This town was originally built around the small church of Sant Lluís that stands out among the rest of the small white houses that make up this town which still today retains its royal French seal on the church façade. Another of the interesting buildings in this tranquil town is the windmill, beautifully restored and which today houses a small ethnological museum that can be visited. On the road that links Sant Lluís and Maó, there is a racecourse and an a flying club.

Sant Lluís

The construction of the church of Sant Lluís was started by the French during their short period of domination of the island. The church was completed under the British and Spanish dominations. On its façade you can see the sculpted caption "A Sant Luis dedicaron este templo los franceses" (This temple was dedicated to Sant Luis by the French).

The rectilinear street layout of the roads of Sant Lluís reveal its short past. The homes built
for farm workers who worked on surrounding **llocs** have maintained their appearance even though they have lost their rural function.

B *The church of Sant Lluís*

The town of Sant Lluís is surrounded by small farmhouses whose names remind us of the Muslim past of the island. These farmhouses are much sought-after as summer holiday homes.

Sant Lluís

The eastern area of Sant Lluís has various exits to the coast. It is an area with much history and one of the first areas to develop tourism. The **La Illa de l'Aire** and it's pretty lighthouse are part of the southernmost territory of Minorca.

Following a path from **s'Algar**, one of the most characteristic in Minorca, you reach **Cala Rafalet** where one of the few gullies in the area culminates.

2 *Cala Rafalet*

The islet of **Es Torn** seems to protect the mouth of **Cala Alcaufar**, a typical fishing village whose foundations touch the sea. This spot was used by Anglo-Dutch troops to disembark at the start of the first British domination. A visit to the defence tower that encloses the cove is recommended. This offers excellent views of the coast.

3 *Alcalfar*

The beach of **Punta Prima** is the sandiest in the area. The English called it "sandy bay". This beach, which is much frequented by the islanders, was one of the first tourist points of interest in the area. From its shore you can make out the **Illa de l'Aire** and its lighthouse.

4 *Punta Prima*

Sant Lluís

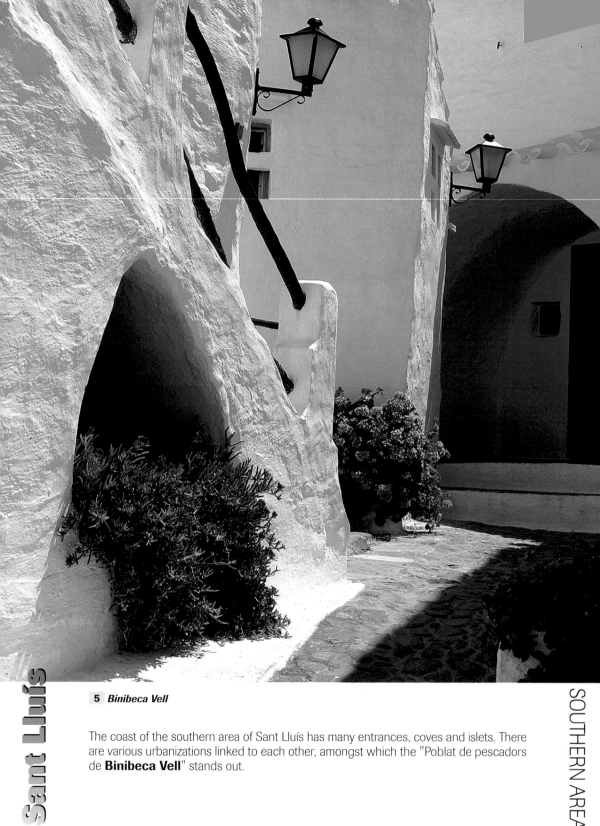

5 *Binibeca Vell*

The coast of the southern area of Sant Lluís has many entrances, coves and islets. There are various urbanizations linked to each other, amongst which the "Poblat de pescadors de **Binibeca Vell**" stands out.

From the urbanization of **Punta Prima** we can reach Cala **Biniancolla**. The original centre of this urbanization is made up of picturesque little houses located on the water's edge of the sea, allowing them to be used for storing small boats.

6 *Biniancolla*

The beach of **Binisafúller** is another choice for enjoying the sun and the sea in this area. The areas around this beach are mainly occupied by villas which means that this urbanization is not too exploited by tourism. From its sandy beach you can make out the islet of the same name. It is one of the biggest in the area.

7 *Binisafúller*

The beach of **Binibeca** is one of the most popular in the area because of its size and the quality of its sand. The small cape of **Morro de en Xua** protects the beach from swells and makes its an ideal spot for swimming.

8 *Platja de Binibeca*

Sant Lluís

9 Cala Torrent

Cala Torret is another of the characteristic urbanizations in this area. Its narrow cove has a jetty that allows small boats to set off. Despite its small size, this urbanization has all the most important services, such as a pharmacy, a supermarket etc. There is also a small selection of restaurants.

1 *Illa de l'Aire*

The **Illa de l'Aire** and its lighthouse are one of the typical scenes of Minorca. This islet is of great ornithological importance being the first point on the island where migratory birds come to rest after their long journeys. The colony of **sargantanes** (endemic lizards of a vivid dark colour) is also important.

ILLA DE L'AIRE *Sant Lluís*

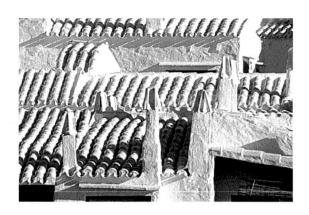

The urbanization of **Binibeca Vell** is without doubt the most picturesque in Minorca. Built in 1968, its structure is based on a typical fishing village. The urbanization keeps to a strict line in all its architecture. The narrow streets are surprising and invite one to take a stroll through them. Strolling through these streets you come across a tiny chapel that seems to indicate the centre of this village. Even though it seems incredible, no fishermen have ever lived here! A jetty has been built on its shore that allows small boats to go out to sea.

11 *Binisafullet*

Taking the **s'Ullestrar** road
from Sant Lluís you reach
the prehistoric settlement
of **Binisafullet**. Here there are
typical elements of Minorcan
settlements such as a taula
(restored), a small **talaiot**,
remains of talaiotic dwellings
and a hypostyle halll. All
these buildings are enclosed
by a wall.

11 *Binisafullet*

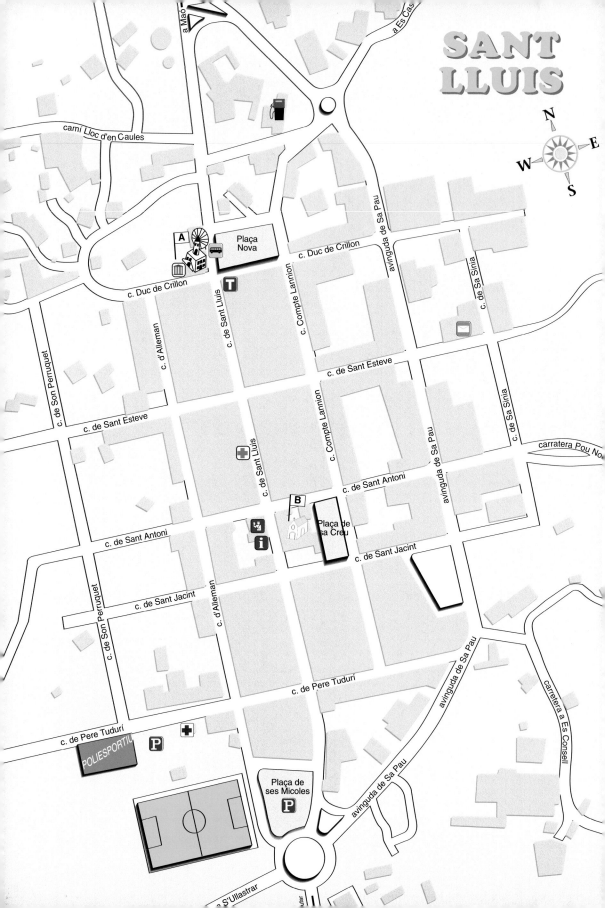

Es Clot d'en Mora
Cap Negre

ES MURTAR

CALA LLONGA

MAÓ

St Antoni

Cala Rata

Cala Figuera

Illa del Rei

Cala Llonga

Cala Corb

Els Escullots

Ses Àguiles

Ses Bancades

Es Freus

Ses Pedres Blaves

Punta de s'Esperó

Cala Corb

Cales Fonts

Illa del Llatzaret

La Mola

HORIZONTE SON VILAR

Trepucó

Son Tudiri

Son Biali

STA ANNA

SOL DE L'ESTE

Na Negra James

Cap de la Mola

Punta d'Es Clot

Bintalfa Vell

Na Xenxa

Binimaimó

ST FELIP

Punta de Sant Carles

Biniarroca

St Llorenç

St Esteve
St Joan

Cala de St Esteve

Son Antoni

Toraixer

FORT DE MARLBOROUCH
TORRE DEN PENJAT

S'Esbrufador

Caló des Vi Blanc

Binifadet

Pou Nou

Ses Cometes

Trebalú

Binissaida

Es Barracons

Na Girada

Rafalet Vell

Binissaida

Sa Cigonya

Es Consell

Rafaletó

So n'Aritger

Son Vidal

Rafalet

Es Sòtil

Camp Sarc

S'Olivera

Son Bonaventura

Racó d'Es Rafalet

Biniancolla

S'ALGAR

S'ALGAR

Alcaufar

Punta des Rafalet

Sa Rinconada

Cala d'Alcaufar

Son Remei

PUNTA PRIMA

Son Ganxo

Platja de Punta Prima

Punta Prima

Sandy Bay

Legend:

240 m.	-10 m.	Main road
200 m.	-20 m.	Secondary road
160 m.	-40 m.	Urban areas
120 m.	-70 m.	Pedestrian path
80 m.	-100 m.	Petrol estation
40 m.	-130 m.	Lighthouse
0 m.		Fishing harbour

Water sports
Yacht club
Defence tower
Beach
Traditional architecture
Windmill
Chapel

Panoramic view
Camp site
Marismas
Wood areas
Ruins
Talaiot
Farmhouses

Taula
Naveta
Caves
Ancient well
Prehistoric settlement

Castell

Island of Minorca

ES CASTELL

Es Castell, the most eastern town in Minorca and consequently in Spain, took its name from es Castell de **Sant Felip**, an old fort that guarded the entrance of the port of Maó. The urban configuration of the town is practically a square grid, its centre being the **s'Esplanada** square. One of the sides of this square is occupied by the town hall building, with its distinctive colonial style red façade. The other sides of the square are occupied by old military barracks, now in disuse. In one of these barracks, that of **Cala Corb**, a military museum is housed that exhibits, among other curiosities, a model of the castle of **Sant Felip**. Another of these historic buildings is the **El Roser** church whose lower floors are occupied by a large ossuary.

A *S'Esplanada*

Es Castell TOWN CENTRE

The **s'Esplanada** square is the nerve-centre of the town. The façade of the town hall is crowned by a small tower built during the times of British domination, when the town was known as Georgetown.

B *Esglèsia del Roser*

On this page we can see different aspects of **Cales Fonts**, whose name was given to it because of the springs that used to flow into its shores. Its shores combine a typically seafaring past with tourist shops and restaurants that cater for the large number of visitors to this small harbour.

On the banks of the jetty there are many Minorcan boats moored and these are called **llaüts**. There are also some larger boats that offer cruises in the vicinity of the town.

A walk along the jetty offers excellent views of the entrance of Maó's harbour. At the end of the bay you can see the island of **Llatzaret**, behind which rises the military peninsula of **La Mola**, which is on the opposite side of the harbour.

1 *Cala Padera*

This area of Es Castell is of great historical value as here there are forts that guarded the entrance of the highly valued port of Maó. Other important buildings include some defence towers that acted as watchtowers as they were situated as continuations of the forts.

Upon leaving the town, the first beach you come across is **Cala Padera**. The surrounding area has been developed into an urbanization called Sol del Est, that reaches the outskirts of the cemetery.

1 *Cala Padera*

The only important inlet in Es Castell 's area is **Cala Sant Esteve**. Flanked by the **Sant Felip** and **Fort Marlborough** forts, this cove, surrounded by old houses, was the key that opened the entrance to the port of Maó.

2 *Cala Sant Esteve*

Typically Mediterranean houses occupy the banks of Cala **Sant Esteve** that for many years have been used as holiday homes.

Es Castell

3 Sant Felip

Turning left from the cemetery of Es Castell there is a short road that takes you to the military zone of **Sant Felip**.

The ruins of this fort, which in days gone by was one of the most important in the Mediterranean, are hardly noticeable and it is only from the air that the star shape of this fortification can be appreciated. Built in 1554 on the orders of Philip II, its basement hid a series of tunnels that communicated with other fortifications. The castle passed into Spanish hands in 1781 and was destroyed under orders of Carlos the III.

4 Fort de Marlborough

Fort Marlbourough, situated on the southern bank of Cala **Sant Esteve**, is one of the not be missed places to visit in Minorca. This fort, built by the English in 1710, took its name from Sir John Churchill, Duke of Marlborough, better known as Mambrú. Carefully restored and open to the public some years ago, its labyrinth of tunnels offers visitors an audiovisual show. In the vicinity of the fort there is Stuart Tower, nicknamed **Torre de en Penjat** (hanged), as this was where convicted men were executed.

ES CASTELL

N · E · S · W

c. des Port
Bellavista
c. des Port
c. Angel Ruiz i Pablo
Sant Ignasi
c. de Sa Font
Ptge.Sta. Àgueda
c. des Port
Miranda de Carles Fonts
Moll de Cales Fonts
c. de Cales Fonts
costa de Cales Fonts
C
c. de Llevant
c. Xaloc
c. Gregal
Tramuntana
c. Llebeig
Ponent
c. de Sant Jaume
c. de Cales Fonts
Sant Alexis
c. de Crilion
Bellavista
c. des Port
c. Victoria
c. Batlle Pons
Miranda de Cala Corb
Moll de Cala Corb
c. de Cales Fonts
c. de Stuart
c. Gran
Padera
Sant Josep
Plaça Constitució
A
Plaça de s'Esplanada
c. de Sant Felip
c. Cala
Victoria
c. Religió
B
Plaça s'Arraval Vella
a Sant Lluis
c.Xisco de Barbaret
c. de Sant Jordi
c. Sant Bernadi
c. de Stuart
c. Victoria
Plaça del Joan Carles I
costa Cala Corb
c. Fàbregues
c. Gran
c. del Rosari
c. de Maó
c. de can Pere Jaume
POLESPORTIU
c. Carles III
c. Ciutadella
c. Bon Aire
c. Sant Cristòfol
c. Santa Bàrbara
c. de Stuart
c. Gran
c. Antonia Ortila
c. de Sant Jordi
c. del Rosari
c. de Maó
costa Moll l'Hospital
c. Fontanilles
c. Agamenón
Camí Vell
c. Fontanilles
carretera de Maó a Es castell a Sant Lluis
camí de sa Granja
cami Nou de Trepucó
a Maó

DIRECTORY

Useful telephone numbers

Emergencies 112
Hospital emergencies 061
Airport 971 157000
National police 091
Trasmediterránea ferries 971 366050
Tourist information office 971 363790
Taxis Maó.................................... 971 367111
Taxis Ciutadella 971 482222
Military Government (visits) 971 362300

For further information on leisure activities, museums, water sports etc., please call:
971 382396.

Buses

Maó - Ciutadella:
8 - 10 - 11,30 - 13 - 16,30 - 19
Ciutadella - Maó:
8 - 10 - 11,30 - 14,30 - 16,30 - 19

Sundays and bank holidays

Maó - Ciutadella:
9 - 11 - 16,30 - 19
Ciutadella - Maó:
9 - 11 - 14,30 - 19

Stops in:
Alaior, es Mercadal y Ferreries

Agrotourism

Biniatram.
Km 1, camino de Algaiarens, carretera de cala Morell. Ciutadella 971 38 31 13

Lloc de Sant Tomàs.
Camí Vell, Km 3. Ciutadella... 971 18 80 51

Bini-Said.
Carretera Cala Galdana. Ferreries. .... 971 15 50 63 - 971 15 50 78

Son Triay Nou.
Carretera Cala Galdana. Ferreries. .... 971 36 04 46 - 971 15 50 78

Llucmaçanes Gran.
Es Pla de Sant Gaietà nº 10. Llucmaçanes, Maó. 971 35 21 17

Alcaufar Vell.
Carretera Alcalfar Km 7,3. Sant Lluís. 971 15 18 74

Sant Joan de Binissaida.
Camí de Toraixa. Es Castell.

Country Hotels

Sant Ignaci. Carretera cala Morell, Km 1. Ciutadella.............................. 971 38 55 75
Biniarroca. Camí de Biniarroca nº 57. Sant Lluís. 971 15 00 59
Hostal Biniali. Carretera s'Ullestrar. Binibeca. Sant Lluís. 971 15 17 29

Hotels

Hotel Patricia. Paseo Sant Nicolau, 90-92. Ciutadella............................ 971 38 55 11
Hotel Géminis. Josepa Rossinyol, 4. Ciutadella....................................... 971 15 00 59
Hotel Playa Grande. Obispo Juano, 2. Ciutadella................................. 971 38 24 45
Hotel l'OAR. Rvdo. Pare Huguet, 1. Ferreries...................................... 971 37 38 88
Hotel Port Mahón. Avinguda Fort de l'Eau, 3. Maó 971 36 26 00
Hotel Capri. San Esteban, 8. Maó.. 971 36 14 00

Restaurants and Pizzerias

Rte. La Guitarra. Carrer dels Dolors, baixos. Ciutadella......................... 971 38 13 55
Rte. Sa Figuera. Puerto de Ciutadella... 971 38 21 12
Rte. Ca Es Ferrer. Portal de Sa Font, nº 16. Ciutadella 971 48 07 84
Café Balear. Puerto de Ciutadella.. 971 38 00 05
Rte. Maribel. Urb. Cala Blanca. Ciutadella 971 38 57 57
Rte. La Mamma. Conqueridor, s/n. Ciutadella 971 48 15 97
Rte. El Gallo. Carretera de Ferreries a Cala Galdana 971 37 30 39
Pizzería Don Giacomo. Carrer Nou de juliol, nº 5. Ciutadella 971 38 32 79
Pizzería Al Capone. Dormidor de Ses Monges, nº 4. Ciutadella 971 38 63 58
Rte. Can Aguedet. Lepanto, nº 30. Es Mercadal.................................. 971 37 53 92
Rte. Es Molí des Es Racó. Carretera Maó - Ciutadella. Es Mercadal ... 971 37 53 92
Rte. Ets Arcs. Carretera Maó - Ciutadella. Es Mercadal 971 37 55 38
Rte. S'Àncora. Passeig Marítim, 7 - 8. Fornells 971 37 66 70
Rte. Marés. Carrer Pont de Es Castell, nº 8. Maó.................................... 971 36 95 76
Rte. La Minerva. Moll de Llevant, nº 87. Maó.. 971 35 19 95
Rte. Itake. Moll de Llevant, nº 317. Maó 971 35 45 70
Rte. Es Molí de Foc. Carrer Sant Llorenç, 65. Sant Climent
Rte. La Rueda. Sant Lluí, nº 30. Sant Lluís.. 971 15 11 84

Bars and Discos

Lateral. Puerto de Ciutadella
Esfera. Puerto de Ciutadella
Jazz–Bah. Puerto de Ciutadella
Gurugú. Es Mercadal
Bar Canya. Alaior
Cova de En Xoroi. Cala en Porter
Akelarre. Puerto de Maó. Moll de Llevant 41-43
Mambo. Puerto de Maó
Iguana. Cala Blanca

Shopping in Minorca

Huit. Carrer Marina, 73-75. Ciutadella. Antiques and gifts.
Castillo Menorca. Carretera Ciutadella-Maó Km 9. Gifts and Lladró china.
Centre Ferreries. Polígono Industrial de Ferreries. Shoes, leather goods and gifts.
Sa Farinera. Outskirts of Es Mercadal. Shopping Centre.
Centro comercial Penya de s'Indi. Outskirts of Es Mercadal. Leather goods and gifts.
Museo del queso Mahón-Sant Patrici. Camí Ruma, s/n. Ferreries. 971 37 37 02
Maribel. Ciutadella, Cala Blanca, Sa Caleta, Calan Bosc. Gifts.

Car hire

Autos Ciutadella. Negrete, 27. Ciutadella 971 48 00 24
Autos Nuracar. Ciutadella.. 971 38 85 64
Rent a car Betacar. Central. Maó 971 36 06 20

Boat charter /Boat trips

Juny 99. Marina, 66. Ciutadella. Boat charter 971 48 21 86

El Pirata Azul. Maó.
Trips round Maó harbour.

Catamaranes Amarillos. Maó.
Departures near the ses Voltes steps.

Don Joan. Maó. Trips round Maó harbour.
Departures near the ses Voltes steps.